Word Games

at Key Stage 2

IMPROVING LITERACY: CREATIVE APPROACHES

Word Games

at Key Stage 2

Alan Peat

Nash Pollock
Publishing

© Alan Peat

First published 2002

Published by
Nash Pollock Publishing
32 Warwick Street
Oxford OX4 1SX

10 9 8 7 6 5

Orders to:
York Publishing Services
64 Hallfield Road
Layerthorpe
York YO31 7ZQ

A catalogue record of this book is available from the British Library.

ISBN: 978 1 898255 41 5

Design and typesetting by Black Dog Design, Buckingham
Printed in Great Britain by The Cromwell Press Group, Trowbridge

Acknowledgements and dedication

The production of this book would not have been possible without the help of numerous individuals who have offered their kind support since the formation of my educational consultancy company. I would like to single out Linda Turner, Chris Pickup, Sue Haywood, Margaret McNeil and Peter Freeman for their sustained, selfless support, assistance and (most important) friendship.

I would also like to thank my father for a list of things far too numerous for such a short dedication. His suggestions, editing skills, and 'liquid refreshment' provision have contributed enormously to the production of this volume.

Contents

Introduction

In his foreword to the National Literacy Strategy Framework (NLF) the then Secretary of State, David Blunkett, correctly drew attention to the disadvantages which result for pupils who do not master the basic skills of literacy. As teachers we need to utilise a broad range of approaches to ensure that the maximum number of pupils not only become functionally literate but also grow into adults who regard literacy as an intrinsic, pleasurable aspect of their lives. Word games are one of the keys to developing an emergent love of literacy. They also provide an inherently enjoyable way of facilitating many of the objectives outlined in the National Literacy Framework.

One of the advantages of a great number of the games included in this book is that they are also readily usable in the wider curriculum. This breadth of possible usage is a feature of the game-based approach to literacy that should commend it to teachers – objectives which are initially covered within the literacy hour can easily be revisited in other curricular contexts. They also make excellent lesson openers – the 'Staircase' game, for example, is an ideal activity to use at the beginning of a lesson whilst also proving useful for gauging prior knowledge if used without books, or for gauging information retrieval skills if used with books. The main reason for producing a book of word games is, however, that they help children to perceive writing as a pleasurable activity – they encourage pupils to play with words!

As educators it is absolutely essential that we allow pupils to experience this pleasure. It does not stem from 'death-by-worksheet' drilling or from a narrowly conceived 'coverage' model of the curriculum and yet it would be unwise to ignore the objectives which are presented in the NLF. For this reason the games included in this volume have all been linked to NLF objectives which are specified after each activity description.

It is important to note that the specified NLF year and term reference should not dissuade teachers from playing the game in a different year or term altogether. The readiness and maturation level of pupils with whom the teacher is working with is the most important factor when deciding the appropriateness of a game's introduction.

All the activities have been selected on the basis of their potential for enhancing pupils' understanding of an aspect (or aspects) of literacy. They have also been chosen on the basis of personal preference – all have been 'tried and tested' by the author and any that already may be familiar are described in terms of approaches that can be utilised.

For ease of reference the games are presented in order of the NLF year and term objective that they facilitate. They do not form any kind of scheme of work, but rather they represent a way of enriching the literacy-experience of Key Stage 2 pupils. The premise upon which this book is based is that, as a profession, we are more likely to achieve educational targets if we make the process of educating and being educated an enjoyable one. Word games are a helpful way of enthusing children and if the motivation to write is intrinsic rather than extrinsic then we will be well on the way to ensuring that our pupils are experiencing the elusive 'excitement factor' when they are writing. Engendering a sense of wonder in the classroom makes a real difference to children's lives – something that must not be lost in our drive to 'cover' objectives.

Questions for Answers

Main idea

To help to embed the concept of questions in a problem-solving manner

How long?

20–30 minutes

National Literacy Strategy links

Year 3 Term 1 S6: 'to secure knowledge of question marks and exclamation marks in reading, understand their purpose and use appropriately in own writing'

Year 5 Term 3 S4: 'to use punctuation marks accurately in complex sentences'

Group size

Pairs

Equipment

Pen; paper; collection of books about the chosen subject

Introduction

In this game pupils are provided with a series of answers for which they have to produce questions. Regardless of subject matter this is a useful game for checking pupils' comprehension of material taught as well as their understanding of the use of question marks.

A dramatic introduction along the following lines works well:

Teacher: 'Today I will not be asking you any questions at all. Instead I've decided to provide you with some answers. Here they are ... 'X', 'Y', 'Z'. Now what I want you to do is to write some questions that go with these answers.'

How to play

To help the children get started the teacher introduces a simple word like 'five' and asks, 'The answer is five. What are the questions?'

Questions are written up and the teacher may wish to model a hierarchy of question types, e.g.:

Type A question (*easy*): What is one more than four? What is one less than six?

Type B question (*harder*): If I have ninety sweets and eat eighty five how many will I have left?

Type C question (*really difficult*): What number, when multiplied by itself, makes a number ten less than thirty five?

(Please note that the questions need not be mathematical.)

Pupils can be asked to aim for type C as these are usually structurally more complex. This also motivates the pupils and demonstrates high expectation on the part of the teacher.

The teacher then provides 10–20 answers, and in a deadlined period they produce questions aiming for type C.

The winners have the most complex questions.

Extension activity

As an extension activity the game can be played in a subject specific context: e.g. when teaching the Tudors, 'The answers are: Farthingale; Henry VIII; Holbein; Ruff and Broken Consort. What are the questions?') Always ensure that books are provided which include the information required, to give an opportunity to reinforce information retrieval skills.

Calligram Challenge

Main idea

To extend vocabulary in a range of subject-specific contexts

How long?

30 minutes

National Literacy Strategy links

If calligrams are produced according to these strict rules the objective link is with *Year 3 Term 1 T13:* 'to invent calligrams and a range of shape poems, selecting appropriate words and careful presentation ...'

Year 5 Term 2 W9: 'to search for, collect, define and spell technical words derived from work in other subjects'

Group size

2–4

Equipment

Pen, paper, tracing paper, paper clips

Introduction

Strictly speaking a calligram is a poem in which the words, letters, or font of the poem represent an aspect of the poem's subject, e.g. a poem about a haunted house may have a shaking font to represent fear. Likewise a poem about growing up may be made up of words which gradually grow in size.

The Calligram Challenge is a variation of the strict calligram form and encourages children to make a picture made up of repeated words, which form the shapes of objects, rather than drawings.

How to play

The pupils are given an outline drawing on A3 paper of something related to work being undertaken in class, e.g. if they have been studying 'Food and Drink' a drawing of a table setting, such as this, could be provided.

They are then given 10 minutes (in groups of 2–4) in which to list as many things as they can see on the drawing, e.g. knife, fork, eggs, plate, sausage.

After the time has elapsed suggestions are then shared and written large for all to see – it is however important to elicit correct spellings.

Questioning by the teacher should then be used to refine the list. If we start with a knife we could ask questions to elicit the component parts of this utensil – the blade and the handle. Similar questioning for the egg should result in the white and yolk being identified.

Using a paperclip a piece of tracing paper is now held in place over the outline drawing. The children are then asked to write the name of one of the objects repeatedly over its outline so that if a fork was chosen the word *fork* would be repeated to form the shape of the fork. The finished example gives an indication of what can be expected.

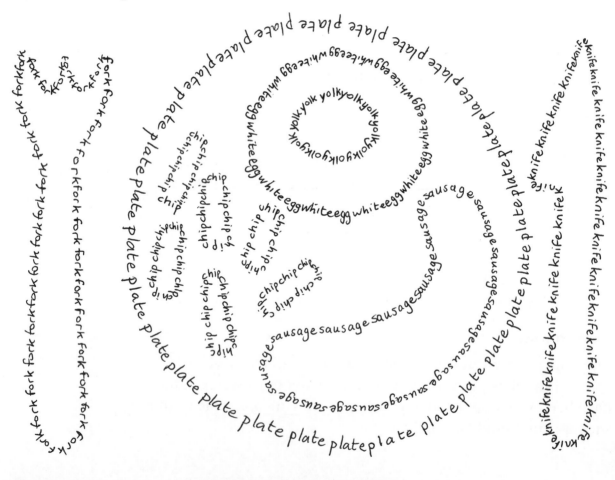

Now that the process has been modelled the Calligram Challenge can be played in a range of contexts. (It can be helpful in relation to spelling development as it helps pupils to associate visual images with written words.) The approach has been used

6

successfully with Year 7 science groups when it has been necessary to familiarise them with names and spellings of unfamiliar equipment such as conical flasks and bunsen burners.

Winning groups are defined as those who add the most words to a given outline drawing (one point is awarded for each word included).

Just a Bunch of Aliens

Main idea

To understand and invent collective nouns

How long?

30–40 minutes

National Literacy Strategy links

Year 3 Term 2 S4c: 'understanding the term 'collective noun' and collecting examples – experiment with inventing other collective nouns'

Group size

Groups of 4

Equipment

Pen; paper; list of collective nouns

Introduction

This game encourages pupils to invent collective nouns and thereby increase their understanding of them.

How to play

The game is introduced by asking 'What do you call a lot of … ?' questions, e.g.

'What do you call a lot of fish?' (A *shoal* of fish)

'What do you call a lot of sheep?' (A *flock* of sheep)

Pupils are divided into groups of four and asked to work together to see how many collective nouns (like *shoal* or *flock*) they can think of.

After 7–8 minutes the outcomes are pooled before introducing a number of unusual examples which complement those provided by the class. A useful list of collective nouns is provided on page 10.

Now that the class has an understanding of what constitutes a collective noun the game can be introduced by explaining that, in groups, they are going to invent collective nouns for a range of different things which the teacher provides. (To ensure an enthusiastic response you should 'think weird' when producing the range of subjects. Good examples include – Angry Aliens; Tired Teachers; Wastebins; Jellies; Lightbulbs.)

The teacher can decide whether or not to allow invented words (neologisms) as well as words retrieved from the dictionary. Both have their advantages but it is best to ask for a definition of any made-up word so that the pupils' thinking is transparent, e.g. 'A wullooboollooboll of jellies': the word is like the shape they all make as they wobble together!

The pupils then have a time limit (approximately 20–30 minutes) to write down their collective nouns for the list the teacher has provided.

The most exciting or inventive examples 'win' and are displayed.

COLLECTIVE NOUNS

Collective noun	Noun
A/an	*of*
Army	soldiers
Atlas	maps
Battery	tests
Brood	chickens
Choir	angels
Clutch	eggs
Colony	ants
Crowd	people
Deck	cards
Embarrassment	riches
Fleet	ships
Flock	sheep
Gaggle	geese
Herd	cows
Litter	puppies
Pack	wolves
Pride	lions
Quiver	arrows
Range	mountains
School	fish
Squadron	planes
Swarm	bees
Suite	rooms
Tribe	monkeys
Wealth	information

Beheadings

Main idea

To help pupils to understand how to spell by analogy

How long?

50 minutes–1 hour

National Literacy Strategy links

Year 3 Term 2 W6d: 'spelling by analogy with other known words, e.g. *light, fright*'

Group size

2–4

Equipment

Pen; paper; dictionaries

Introduction

'I'm in the mood for a beheading!' – an introductory sentence which usually serves to focus the attention of pupils involved in this word game. The object is to find, in a limited time, as many words as possible which can be beheaded to leave another word.

How to play

The teacher writes examples of words that can be beheaded on the board. Examples of such words include:

Crag (which becomes *rag*)

Dover (which becomes *over*)

Bright (which becomes *right*)

The pupils are then asked to get rid of (behead) the first letter from each word and by writing these up on a suitable surface the pupils will see that what remains in each case is an acceptable word.

Pupils are then given a limited time (25–30 minutes) in which to find as many beheadable words as possible.

When the time has elapsed, the teacher instigates a discussion regarding methods of maximimizing the number of beheadings within the time limit. (It is better to draw this from the pupils rather than explicitly teach it.) Pupils often suggest ways of increasing their word count, such as the addition of plurals, e.g. *crag – rag* becomes *crags – rags*. The addition of the letter 'y' to the end of words is sometimes offered as another tactic. Hence *hair – air* becomes *hairy – airy*. After this discussion pupils spend a further 10–20 minutes finding further beheadable words.

A 'winning' group is then chosen.

Extension activities

An alternative to the above is to give pupils a section of text (which must be checked beforehand as it is surprisingly easy to choose a page from a book which is devoid of beheadable words) and ask them to find as many beheadable words as possible. Better still, you can tell them how many you have found and encourage them to beat your attempt, thereby setting up a motivational challenge. As long as it isn't too obvious, subtracting one or two from your real score can give children a tremendous sense of achievement when they 'win'!

Another strategy to fulfil the same objective is to play *Curtailments*.

This game is played in the same manner as 'Beheadings', but in this instance pupils have to find words which can be curtailed, rather than beheaded, to form a new word.

Thus when curtailed:

   damp becomes *dam*,

   done becomes *don*

   inn becomes *in*.

For the teacher who wishes to vary the approach already taken when playing 'Beheadings' an additional strategy is to ask pupils to find the longest and shortest words that can be curtailed. It would be wise to ban plurals when asking for the longest curtailment!

Staircase

Main idea

To extend pupils' vocabulary and to improve spelling

How long?

20–30 minutes

National Literacy Strategy links

Year 3 Term 2 W6e: 'using word banks, dictionaries'

Group size

Pairs

Equipment

Pen; paper

Introduction

'Staircase', like 'Rally' (see page 73), is an effective brainstorming activity.

How to play

The teacher selects a theme and a word related to that theme, e.g. *Vegetable: carrot.*

Then ask the children to produce a staircase of words, beginning with *carrot*, all of which are related to the theme of vegetable.

The teacher may wish to ask 'What does *carrot* end with?' After eliciting the answer then a further question, 'So, can anyone think of a vegetable beginning with 't'?' may be asked. As each answer is given the teacher models the staircase for all to see. Thus

```
C a r r o t
        u
        r
        n
        i
        p o t a t o
                n
                i
                o
                n
```

If the pupils experience difficulty in finding appropriate words the teacher can demonstrate/remind the pupils how to retrieve information from books related to the theme.

Now that the process has been modelled, pupils are divided into pairs and asked to produce their own staircase in a given period of time.

The winning pair produces a staircase with the most words within the time limit.

(N.B. To avoid copying words without any understanding of their meaning, it should be stressed that the meaning of any word used must be known – this can be tested!)

Alphabet Sentences

Main idea

To consolidate dictionary skills and use these to a purposeful end

How long?

20–30 minutes

National Literacy Strategy links

Year 3 Term 2 W19: 'to use dictionaries to learn or check the spellings and definitions of words'

Group size

2–4

Equipment

Pen; paper; dictionaries

Introduction

The aim of 'Alphabet Sentences' is to produce a sentence from words beginning with each letter of the alphabet in alphabetical order. Although this game is very hard to complete the author has found that if it is introduced as a 'game' then the challenge intrigues rather than frustrates pupils.

How to play

Pupils are divided into groups of 2–4.

The teacher explains that the purpose of the game is to produce a sentence using words that begin with each letter of the alphabet … in order! Any letter can be chosen as the starting point.

The following modelled example is shared with the pupils after the teacher explains they have begun with the letter 'c'.

Can dust ever freeze?

The teacher then explains that this would score 4 points as it has words beginning with C, D, E and F.

The pupils are then invited to try their own alphabet sentences. (Can they beat the teacher's score of 4?)

Extension activitites

The pupils can produce their own alphabet sentence starters using letters a–d. These are then passed to a different group who use the letters e–h to extend the sentence and so on until the sentence is complete.

For more able pupils, putting words in alphabetical lists could be banned.

Pupils could also be invited to try and continue sentences, for example:

THE HUNGRY CAT
A big cat devours eggs, flour, …

COLIN'S TERRIBLE DAY
After breakfast Colin dropped …

(The pupils can be reminded to use commas to separate items in a list.)

The Dictionary Game

Main idea

To write to a given structure

How long?

10–20 minutes

National Literacy Strategy links

Year 3 Term 2 W19: 'to use dictionaries to learn or check spellings and definitions of words'

Year 3 Term 2 W20: 'to write their own definitions of words, developing precision and accuracy in expression'

Year 5 Term 2 W9: 'to search for, collect, define and spell technical words derived from work in other subjects'

Group size

2–4

Equipment

Pen; paper; collection of books about the chosen subject

Introduction

This is a simple word game in which two teams of pupils compete to guess words (beginning with a specified letter) from their definitions. It never fails to captivate pupils and can create enthusiasm for dictionary use. If concentration wanes I recommend that the teacher selects definitions which ensure that the teams are evenly matched.

How to play

The class is divided into two teams.

A scorer is then appointed from each team and a coin is tossed to decide which team will select a letter of the alphabet. (If the game is played regularly an alphabet line should be included in the environment and as a letter is chosen it can be crossed out. Only letters which are not crossed out can then be chosen, thus ensuring variety over time.)

When the letter has been selected, the teacher turns to that letter and reads the first team a definition of a word beginning with it.

If the first team provides the correct word for the definition, then they score a point.

The second team are then given their definition and so on. (Should either team fail then the other team are given the opportunity to provide the correct word and thus score a bonus point.)

Extension activities

Variations on the above method include (a) giving extra points for the correct spelling of the word (b) asking each team to prepare their own definitions for a range of words (c) themed definition challenges.

Themed challenges are useful ways of assisting pupils to remember key information from any subject area. A subject-specific definition is given first and pupils have to state the key word to which it pertains. This method makes the acquisition of subject-specific key words more interesting for the pupils.

Same Letter Sentences (Tautograms)

Main idea

To facilitate effective dictionary use through a game

How long?

10–15 minutes

National Literacy Strategy links

Year 3 Term 2 W22: 'to know the quartiles of the dictionary, e.g. *m* lies around the halfway mark, *t* toward the end'

Group size

Groups of 4 (smaller groups are not advised as the game is difficult!)

Equipment

Pen; paper; dictionaries

Introduction

A Tautogram is a sentence in which every word begins with the same letter of the alphabet. The aim of the game is to write Tautograms which are as long as possible. The game actively encourages use of a dictionary and, although demanding, is achievable. The aim is to write Tautograms as long as possible.

How to play

The teacher shows the pupils one or two examples of Tautograms to show how they are constructed, e.g.

(a) *Sale shopping's super since saving so spectacularly seems splendid.*
(b) *To teach tiny tots takes time, tact and tremendous tenderness.*

In the second example one word does not begin with 't'. The teacher points this out and explains that the pupils can use between 1–3 words which do not begin with the chosen letter of the Tautogram.

It is also worth introducing a rule that only two names can be used! This avoids the likes of 'Sam, Steve, Sophie, Samantha and Stephanie sip soda'.

Pupils then choose a letter of the alphabet and, in groups of four, attempt to write as long a Tautogram as possible. Please stress at the beginning that what they write has to make sense.

The most interesting examples are displayed and praised.

Guggenheims

Main idea

To embed second-letter alpha-ordering in a 'games' context

How long?

20 minutes

National Literacy Strategy links

Year 3 Term 2 W23: 'to organise words or information alphabetically, using the first two letters'

Group size

2–4

Equipment

Pen; paper; copy of Guggenheims Grid; computer with Internet access

Introduction

Guggenheims is a game in which a focus word is chosen together with a number of themes. Words are then found for each of these themes, using the individual letters of the focus word. These words are then transferred to a grid. This is essentially a parlour game that is easily translated into the classroom context.

How to play

Pupils are divided into groups of 2–4.

A focus word e.g. HOUSE is chosen and written horizontally along the top of a pre-prepared grid as shown below.

A column of subjects, which need not be related, is then written down the left hand side of the grid. These can be suggested by the pupils or chosen by the teacher. Ask for two suggestions in the first instance.

	H	O	U	S	E
Food					
Pop groups					
Etc					

Once the grid has been produced it is completed by the class/group as on the following page. (In teacher Inset sessions the answers to 'Pop Groups' acts as an indicator of the average age of the staff involved!)

	H	O	U	S	E
Food	Ham	Orange	Ugly Fruit		
Pop groups	Happy Mondays	Oasis	U2		
Etc					

Now that the game has been modelled a further eight subjects are suggested by the class, or added in by the teacher.

The pupils then copy the grid and complete it as above.

The aim is to see how quickly the grid can be completed.

Pupils should be given access to the Internet if they cannot find answers.

Once the grid has been completed the pupils have to create an alphabetic list of words in each column.

The winning group is the first to complete the grid and then to alpha-order each column.

Finally, if the children list the words in each column alphabetically once they have completed the grid, the NLS objective cited above can be achieved.

Extension activity

A subject-specific Guggenheim is a useful extension activity which encourages information retrieval skills. If, for example, the group was studying 'Life and living things' then the subjects in the left hand column could all be related to that theme:

	L	I	V	I	N	G
Animals						
Plants						
Trees						
etc.						

If the pupils have access to a range of books related to 'Life and living things' the Guggenheim can be used to assess the pupils' ability to extract information from a non-fiction book. (A useful tip to share beforehand with the class is that usually words in bold or italics can be found in the glossary. This explicit information, related to a simple typographical device, considerably improves information retrieval.) Access to the Internet is of great use if the pupils have difficulty retrieving information from traditional sources.

Guggenheims Grid

Name _____   Date _____   Title _____

Focus word → Subjects →					

Zoophabets

Main idea

To encourage pupils to write a simple book collaboratively.

How long?

15–20 minutes per page (the book can be completed over a half term)

National Literacy Strategy links

Year 3 Term 3 T15: 'to write poetry that uses sound to create effects, e.g. onomatopoeia, alliteration, distinctive rhythms' (Although the game doesn't have a poem as an end result, it does introduce pupils to alliteration in an effective and memorable manner.)

Group size

Pairs

Equipment

Pen; paper; booklet of 26 Zoophabet pages made from the accompanying photocopiable sheet (the letters of the alphabet should be written in the small box to the top right of the sheet)

Introduction

A Zoophabet is a book produced by pupils which has the following format: each page is devoted to a letter of the alphabet and has a space for a drawing to be included. The following sentence starters are written underneath this space.

I am called …

I eat …

I live in …

This page layout is shown on the accompanying photocopiable sheet.

How to play

The pupils are divided into pairs.

Each pair is provided with the booklet described above.

The teacher then models the letter 'A' page by asking the pupils to suggest a name, food and habitation each of which begins with the letter A, e.g. Alan; Apples; Australia.

The teacher then writes the suggestion on to a large blank template such as the pupils have in their booklet.

The teacher then produces a humorous drawing of Alan eating apples in Australia.

Attention is then drawn to alliteration by joining the pupils' ideas into one alliterative sentence e.g. 'I am called Alan and I eat apples in Australia.'

Now that the process has been modelled the pupils (over several sessions) produce their own collaborative Zoophabets.

Extension activity

The sentence starters indicated in the game description can easily be changed to vary the activity e.g.

I am called …

I like …

I don't like …

or

I am called …

I can …

I can also …

Zoophabets

I am called

I eat

I live in

Trigrams

Main idea

To explore language in a games context

How long?

25 minutes

National Literacy Strategy links

Year 3 Term 3 W6e: 'Using word banks, dictionaries'

Group size

Groups of 3

Equipment

Pen; paper; dictionaries

Introduction

Three consecutive letters, such as *ine*, constitute a Trigram. To play the game pupils have to find as many words as possible which include the three chosen letters, e.g. *Ine*rt, L*ine*, L*ine*r.

How to play

The pupils are divided into groups of 3.

The teacher models Trigams, using information from the introduction. The modelled example *ine* should prove useful in this context.

The pupils are then given five trigrams, selected by the teacher, and given a deadline of approximately 25 minutes in which to complete as many words as possible.

The winners produce the most words which include the trigrams.

Extension activity

Additional challenges can be issued to make the game increasingly complex for more able students. In this case pupils are asked if they can find words that begin or end with the trigram or have it placed centrally. The examples above fulfil these criteria.

The following examples can be used as models.

Trigram *ust*: just, australian, rust, rusting

Trigram *lin*: line, healing, linoleum, crawling, splinter

A Quattrogram is simply an extension of the Trigram as it has four, rather than three, letters. E.g. *wlin*: crawling.

Examples of Trigrams

alk	*par*	*end*	*tho*
alt	*ith*	*oth*	*ver*
ery	*lam*	*ste*	*wal*

Examples of Quadrograms

eigh	*ould*	*tion*	*tive*
ease	*team*	*ates*	*ious*
port	*ment*	*each*	*ight*

Build-a-list

Main idea

To reinforce pupils' understanding of prefixes and/or suffixes

How long?

20–30 minutes (total)

National Literacy Strategy links

Year 3 Term 3 W9: 'to recognise and spell the prefixes: *mis-, non-, ex-, co-, anti-*'

Year 4 Term 1 W9: 'to recognise and spell the suffixes: *-al, -ary, -ic, -ship, -hood, -ness, -ment*'

Year 4 Term 2 W13: 'a range of suffixes that can be added to nouns and verbs to make adjectives, e.g. *wash..able, hope.,ful, shock..ing, child..like, hero..ic, road..worthy*'

Group size

2–4

Equipment

Pen; paper; dictionaries

Introduction

The main object of Build-a-list is to facilitate a situation in which the pupils (through the game) can discuss both the function and meaning of either prefixes or suffixes, and in this sense the game is a means to an end rather than the end itself. The simplest Build-a-list game has the following form.

How to play

The teacher provides the pupils with a prefix (such as *anti-*) or suffix (such as *–ary*).

Without the aid of a dictionary, pupils, working in groups, list as many words as possible beginning with that prefix (or ending with that suffix). The teacher sets a time limit of 10 minutes.

At the end of the allotted time pupils use a dictionary to find additional words beginning with the same prefix, or ending with the same suffix. These are not added to their score but help to form the basis of a discussion of the meaning of the prefix/suffix based on the words the pupils have listed.

Extension activity

A more complex variation of the game is achieved by giving children a noun or a verb and asking them to add as many suffixes as possible, e.g. shock – shocking – shockable.

A list of suffixes and prefixes is included here.

SUFFIXES		PREFIXES	
Suffix	*Example*	*Prefix*	*Example*
able	likeable	bi	bicycle
ed	walked	com	company
er	stronger	con	concert
est	strongest	dis	disobey
ful	careful	en	enjoy
ian	musician	im	improbable
ible	forcible	in	insane
ing	walking	mis	mistake
ist	therapist	non	nonsense
less	careless	pre	preparation
ly	sadly	re	recall
ment	treatment	tri	tricycle
ness	weakness	un	unwrap
ous	dangerous	un	unconscious
or	actor		

Words Instead of 'Said'!

Main idea

To vary pupils' vocabulary in story writing

How long?

10–12 minutes

National Literacy Strategy links

Year 3 Term 3 W13: 'to collect synonyms which will be useful in writing dialogue, e.g. *shouted, cried, yelled, squealed ...*'

Group size

Whole class or group

Equipment

Suitable writing surface upon which to write suggestions

Introduction

This simple, short game can be played before story writing. The class have to suggest as many words as possible to replace the word 'said' in a simple sentence, e.g. 'Mr Smith said "Hello!" '

How to play

The teacher writes the sentence 'Mr Smith said "Hello!" ' on the board for all to see ('Mr Smith' is replaced with the teacher's name).

The teacher then explains that in five minutes the class/group are going to try to suggest more than ten words to replace the word 'said'.

The pupils then write their suggestions on the writing surface.

If they dry up, the teacher should prompt them by performing the sentence in the manner of the missing word, e.g. whispering it, shouting it, mumbling it, screaming it!

When as many suggestions as possible have been made the teacher explains that they should be used and underlined in the story that they are about to write – thereby directly tackling the issue of transferability.

Extension activity

The above process can be repeated with words such as *nice* and *good* which are routinely used in a repetitive manner by pupils. By inventing a sentence containing the word the teacher helps the pupils to see the alternatives in context rather than as isolated words.

Telestich

Main idea

To write to a given structural model

How long?

30–40 minutes

National Literacy Strategy links

Year 4 Term 2 T11: 'to write poetry based on the structure and/or style of poems read, e.g. taking account of vocabulary, archaic expressions, patterns of rhyme, choruses, similes'

Group size

Groups of 3

Equipment

Pen; paper

Introduction

The Telestich is a more complex version of the Acrostic (an Acrostic is a poem in which the initial letters of each line form a word – see page 75).

How to play

To produce a Telestich the teacher first selects a subject word such as 'Food'.

In groups of three the pupils write the word vertically on the right of the page.

They are then given ten minutes to brainstorm words which end with each of the letters which make up the word 'food'. As an example:

F   *....off, of*

O   *....too, to*

O   *....so, no*

D   *....bad, sad*

The suggestions are written for all to see.

The teacher then models how to complete a Telestich by choosing one of the words suggested for each line and using it to end each sentence about the chosen subject.

Food, beyond its sell-by date, may have gone off.

Food, left in the sun, may do so too.

If someone tries to sell you such produce just say 'NO'.

Then tell them that their food is bad.

Now that the process has been modelled the pupils are given a new subject word and between 20–30 minutes in which to complete their Telestich.

The best examples are displayed and/or made into a class book.

Extension activity

An easy variant of the Telestich is the Acrostic (see page 75). A more complex variant is the 'Tele-Acro' in which the letters of the subject word both begin *and* end each line!

Kennings

Main idea

To play with language!

How long?

15–20 minutes

National Literacy Strategy links

Year 4 Term 2 T11: 'to write poetry based on the structure and/or style of poems read, e.g. taking account of vocabulary, archaic expressions, patterns of rhyme, choruses, similes'

Group size

Pairs

Equipment

Pen; paper; dictionaries; photocopy of 'Can you turn these into Kennings?' A–Z sheet

Introduction

A Kenning is usually a compound expression used to represent a name or noun, especially in Old English or Old Norse poetry, e.g. 'storm of swords' is a Kenning for 'battle'.

How to play

Pupils are divided into pairs.

The teacher defines what a Kenning is using the information in the introduction.

Pupils are asked to provide a noun, or the teacher provides a suitable one, e.g. *ship*.

The teacher explains that they are going to produce a Kenning by describing what a ship does. The following is then written on to a suitable writing surface.

–––––*of the*–––––

The teacher then models the process of writing a Kenning by thinking aloud: 'I am now thinking about what a ship does ... It rides the waves ... So Rider of the Waves will work well.'

The teacher then writes the words 'rider' and 'waves' in the spaces left for that purpose and the production of a model Kenning is completed.

The class are then asked to suggest appropriate 'of the' phrases or Kennings, for other nouns, e.g. *Umbrella* becomes 'Fighter of the rain', *Dog* becomes 'Biter of the ankle'.

The teacher demonstrates how all of these can be shortened so that:

Rider of the waves = *Wave rider*

Fighter of the rain = *Rain fighter*

Biter of the ankle = *Ankle biter.*

The pairs are then given a list of nouns to turn into Kennings – a photocopiable sheet is provided after this game description.

A deadline of about 15 minutes is set to increase the motivational level of the pupils.

The winning team can either be the one which produces the most Kennings or the one whose Kennings are the most exciting. (The words can be thematic, and part of the appeal of the game is that it can easily be related to any subject or aspect of the curriculum. When using subject-specific words the game can be used to diagnose pupils' levels of comprehension as it is impossible to write a Kenning for a word which is not understood!)

Extension activity

Pupils, in different pairs, can be asked to write Kennings for nouns beginning with a specific letter (a dictionary should be provided for their use). After 15–20 minutes has elapsed each pair swaps with another and attempts to guess the nouns from which the Kennings have been derived.

Can you turn these into Kennings?

Don't forget... Start by using '_____ *of the* _____' then shorten it.

Word	_____ *of the* _____	Shortened Kenning
ant		
bottle		
cap		
door		
egg		
fence		
glass		
house		
ink		
jar		
kettle		
lamp		
moon		
nest		
oar		
pudding		
queen		
ring		
submarine		
tongue		
umbrella		
vase		
wellingtons		
x-ray		
yo-yo		
zoo		

The Rashomon Effect

Main idea

To write from a range of perspectives and to collaboratively redraft in order to produce a 'finished' piece of writing

How long?

3–5 sessions of 40 minutes (minimum)

National Literacy Strategy links

Year 4 Term 2 T12: 'to collaborate with others to write stories in chapters, using plans with particular audiences in mind'

Year 6 Term 1 T6: 'to manipulate narrative perspective by ... writing a story with two different narrators'

Group size

Groups of 5

Equipment

Pen; paper; dictionaries

Introduction

The Rashomon Effect is simply the same story told from several different perspectives. The game is played in the context of story writing and as such is not a game played with individual words. It is, nevertheless, worthy of inclusion as it invites children to play with language in order to manipulate narrative perspective. It also helps to develop narrative writing skills, particularly the ability to assume an alternate frame of reference (to step into the character's shoes) when producing a story.

How to play

Pupils are divided into groups of five.

The teacher explains the 'Rashomon Effect' along the lines of the introduction.

The teacher creates a dramatic situation which will form the basis of the story. e.g. 'The plane crash'.

It is then explained that each member of the team of five has to take a different person's perspective and write their story from that character's viewpoint. If 'The plane crash' was chosen, five possible viewpoints could be:

(1) The crash told from the pilot's perspective: he/she escapes but is badly burned.

(2) The crash told from a passenger's perspective: he/she escapes but, suffering from smoke inhalation, barely makes it from the plane.

(3) An eyewitness, on the ground, who is deeply shocked by the event.

(4) A relative of a passenger, who has heard about the crash on a television broadcast, but does not know if there are any survivors.

(5) A crash inspector who discovers the cause of the accident.

Pupils are allotted a specific time in which to complete their story. (This game is most successful when taken out of the confines of the Literacy Hour. It is an excellent game to explore in the context of extended writing, perhaps over a number of sessions.)

When each of the five stories has been completed, the team is asked to edit and improve the original drafts. (It may be appropriate for the teacher to discuss refining strategies at this point.)

The pupils are then asked to make the stories into books which are sent to another class for judging. (The teacher may wish to discuss marking criteria with the pupils, e.g. development of characters; excitement; intricacy of plot etc.)

The winning team's book is published and copies are placed in the school and class libraries.

Extension activity

A more complex way of approaching the Rashomon Effect is to ask individual pupils to write all five chapters, thereby assuming multiple perspectives themselves. This approach provides a useful way of differentiating for the more able.

Expansions

Main idea

To play with language within a given structural model

How long?

30 minutes

National Literacy Strategy links

Year 4 Term 2 T13: 'to write own examples of descriptive, expressive language based on those read. Link to work on adjectives and similes'

Group size

2–4

Equipment

Pen; paper; collection of books about the chosen subject

Introduction

Expansions can be played orally or as a writing game. Pupils are either given a word or theme and are asked to expand it by speaking or writing about it. Each time they say or write something new it must be one word longer than the previous statement or piece of writing. As with many other word games developed in this book, modelling the form helps to develop pupil understanding.

How to play

The teacher models how to play Expansions by writing the word 'Wood' on the board and then writing down the following sentences:

It's useful (*two words*)

Comes from trees

You can carve it

It can be set alight

Another word for it is timber

Wood can be used to make furniture

Even small objects, such as toothpicks, are wooden

A wood is not as big as a forest (*nine words*)

The pupils are asked if they can see a pattern. (If it is not immediately obvious to them, ask them to count the words.)

When the pattern has been ascertained, i.e. an extra word for each sentence, the pupils are given two or three theme words for writing their own Expansions.

A deadline is set and if the theme words are subject specific (e.g. Metals), books on the subject are provided.

When the time has elapsed the teacher marks the work, chooses winners and displays their 'Expansions'.

Extension activities

To avoid a repetitive approach, e.g. *it is nice*
it is very nice
it is the very best! (etc.)

pupils should be taught strategies which help them to vary their sentences. One way of doing this is to link the teaching of Expansions to the teaching of similes, e.g. *'It is like a .... '* sentences. A further method of ensuring variety is to ask pupils to think about what it looks like, feels like, smells like, sounds like, what it can be used for, how it is made, etc. The range of prompts will obviously depend upon the theme word but their use ensures that pupils do not get 'stuck' too quickly.

Univocalics

Main idea

To explore language and seek out synonyms or alternative phrases using dictionaries and thesauruses as an aid

How long?

20–30 minutes

National Literacy Strategy links

Year 4 Term 2 W3e: 'using word banks, dictionaries'

Group size

Pairs

Equipment

Pen; paper; dictionaries; thesauruses

Introduction

A Univocalic is a sentence, paragraph or even an entire story or essay which uses only one vowel. Their production demands time but is useful as it actively encourages, and often necessitates, the use of a thesaurus to seek alternatives to words initially thought of. Sentences are harder to produce than dialogue.

We rested when they went. The rest seemed endless. (using 'e')

Writing a playscript is easier:

Character A: Sell me the pen.

Character B: Yes, here.

Character A: Hey, the end's bent!

How to play

The aim of the game is to write as much as possible in a stated period of time. The author finds that 20–30 minutes is about right. As the game is difficult the purpose needs careful articulation.

The pupils are divided into pairs.

Univocalics are defined using the information above.

The single vowel to be used is designated.

Collectively, pupils brainstorm words which can or cannot be used. The teacher writes these on a suitable surface for all to see.

A dramatic countdown marks the beginning of the 'Univocalics Composition'.

The pupils work together for the specified time.

At the end of this time a word count is undertaken and a winning pair is decided upon.

Sentence Substitutions

Main idea

To extend pupils' vocabulary beyond the familiar

How long?

20 minutes

National Literacy Strategy links

Year 4 Term 2 W9: 'to use alternative words and expressions which are more accurate and interesting than the common choices, e.g. *got, nice, good, then*'

Group size

Pairs

Equipment

Pen; paper; thesauruses

Introduction

This is a game which encourages pupils to use livelier words or phrases in place of less powerful words. It can also be used to expand vocabulary and reinforce understanding of synonyms.

How to play

The teacher provides the class with sentences or paragraphs in which some words are underlined.

'A <u>nice</u> man <u>got</u> the ball from the roof where the boy had kicked it. I thought it was a <u>good</u> thing that he had helped, <u>then</u> I thought about what could have happened if the boy had tried himself.' (See the example below for a further passage.)

The pupils then suggest how the passage might be rewritten using more interesting words than those underlined, e.g. 'A *kind* man *fetched* the ball from the roof where the boy had kicked it. I thought it was a *kind-hearted* thing that he had helped, *moreover* I thought about what could have happened if the boy had tried himself.'

The pupils are divided into pairs and given another passage in which a number of words are underlined.

They are told that the object of the game is to change all the underlined words in 15–20 minutes.

The 'winners' make the most suggestions.

Example

Can you make the underlined words more interesting?

It was a <u>cold</u> day when I <u>went</u> to the park to play football. I <u>love</u> playing football because it's a <u>great</u> game. My friends <u>say</u> that they <u>like</u> cricket better but I don't agree.

It <u>began</u> to <u>rain</u> almost <u>straightaway</u>, so I put on my <u>coat</u> and <u>ran fast</u> to the hut at the side of the field. It was a <u>bad</u> place with writing on the walls and a <u>smell</u> of staleness. It wasn't a place where you would <u>stay</u> long.

<u>Luckily</u> the <u>rain</u> ended after only a few minutes so we took our boots out of our <u>bags</u> and we went on to the grass. It was <u>wet</u>. We wouldn't have been <u>happy</u> if we'd <u>fallen</u> on it.

The game was <u>good</u>. We played for the whole morning and then had lunch.

Extension activity

'Improve a Text' is a variation in which the pupils are given a photocopy of a page or two from a book. They then underline for themselves words which could be made more interesting and write their suggestions. The concept of improving an 'already published' book (perhaps by a favourite author) can be used to develop the pupils' sense of *themselves* as effective writers.

Yoked Sentences

Main idea

To write to a given structure

How long?

20–30 minutes

National Literacy Strategy links

Year 4 Term 3 S3: 'to understand how the grammar of a sentence alters when the sentence type is altered ...'

Year 6 Term 1 S5: 'to form complex sentences ...'

Group size

2–4

Equipment

Pen; paper; dictionaries; books about the chosen subject

Introduction

A yoked sentence begins with the last word of the previous sentence. This is best played in pairs with a maximum number of four for each writing group.

How to play

The teacher selects a theme – say 'Animals' – and the pupils are asked to suggest a sentence related to it, e.g. 'Some animals make good pets but others are too vicious.'

The pupils are asked to yoke another sentence to this by beginning it with the word that ended their first sentence (an opportunity for dictionary work presents itself with the word 'yoke'): 'Vicious animals, like lions, certainly would not make good pets.'

The two sentences are 'yoked' by the word *vicious* so that when taken together they read: 'Some animals make good pets but others are too vicious. Vicious animals, like lions, certainly would not make good pets.'

The pattern is continued for two or three more sentences with the stipulation that yoked words must not be repeated after their initial use.

Now that the process has been modelled the groups are given a new theme and related books.

They have 20–30 minutes in which to produce as long a piece of writing as possible, using yoked sentences.

The game encourages the use of different sentence types and can produce surprisingly mature results. It also allows pupils to learn from one another in a structured manner.

Extension activity

A more complex variant is achieved by yoking each new sentence by using the last *two* words of a sentence to form the first *two* words of the following sentence.

Start-of-line Rhyming

Main idea

To experiment with rhyming couplets in an unusual way

How long?

30–40 minutes

National Literacy Strategy links

Year 4 Term 3 T14: 'to write poems, experimenting with different styles and structures, discuss if and why different forms are more suitable than others'

Group size

Pairs

Equipment

Pen; paper

Introduction

Start-of-line rhymes are the opposite of end-of-line rhymes e.g.

End-of-line rhyme:

> I was walking down the street one *day*
> I'd just collected my weekly *pay.*

Start-of-line rhyme:

> *Day* breaks and the sun rises to warm me;
> *Pay* is needed for many things, but not the weather.

How to play

There are numerous ways of playing this game, so a strict sequence is not required.

Firstly pupils, in pairs, can attempt a two-line, start-of-line-rhymed slogan. (The activity can be linked to any work on advertising.) It is useful to provide a model:

> *Chew* me, chew me, never grow tired of my flavour,
> *Through* day and night I always taste great!

The class can be asked to provide alternative first lines for a chewing gum slogan. Words that rhyme with the first word of their suggested lines can then be listed, and be used to produce two-line slogans. Once the concept is understood then they can go on to produce slogans for a range of products.

An alternative way by which pupils will gain an understanding of start-of-line rhymes is to take a short poem which uses end-of-line rhymes and turn it into a start-of-line rhyme poem. Nursery rhymes (or altered nursery rhymes) provide ideal stimulus material for this activity.

End-of-line rhyme

> Mary had a little lamb,
> Its fleece was white as *snow*,
> And everywhere that Mary went
> That lamb was sure to *go*.

Start-of-line rhyme

> *Mary* had a little spider,
> *Hairy* beast it was,
> *She* ran away and left it,
> *We* saw it crying when she'd gone.

Extension activity

Provide pupils with three (or more) rhyming couplets for initial rhyming. A useful set is *space, place, day, say, do, you*. In workshops this sequence usually produces interesting results!

Near-rhyme Games

Main idea

To expand pupils' vocabulary in a word game context

How long?

15 minutes

National Literacy Strategy links

Year 4 Term 3 T14: 'to write poems, experimenting with different styles and structures, discuss if and why different forms are more suitable than others'

Group size

Pairs

Equipment

Pen; paper

Introduction

Near-rhymes consist of words which almost rhyme. As the concept is difficult to grasp it is wise to establish a base-word and then to apply the following rules

Chosen base-word: same

(a) Alter the vowel sound but retain the start and end sound to produce *seem, some, sum,* etc.

(b) Alter the initial sound and vowel sound but retain the end sound to give *time, beam, doom,* etc.

(c) Alter the consonant between the *a...e* split digraph to create *sane, sale, sage,* etc.

How to play

The teacher introduces a base-word (as in the introduction).

The pupils are then told rule (a) from the introduction and are asked to suggest near-rhymes. The rule is written up, together with the suggestions, for all to see.

The pupils are then told rule (b) and are again asked to suggest near-rhymes. This rule, together with suggestions emanating from it, is written for all to see.

Rule (c) is now treated in the same manner.

Now that the process has been modelled, pupils are divided into pairs and given three or four new base-words.

The aim of the game is to produce as many near-rhymes as possible, from each base-word, within a 15 minute period (approximately). It may be appropriate to remind the class that all the rules can be used.

Extension activity

In order to differentiate the game, 'Eye-rhyme' could be played with more able children. An eye-rhyme consists of two or more words which look as though they should rhyme but, when spoken aloud, do not do so.

e.g. *bough – cough; brow – crow; cow – tow; mow – now; near – pear; brown – grown,* etc

The rules are exactly the same as for Near-rhyme.

Xeransis

Main idea

To expand pupils' vocabulary in a word game context

How long?

20–30 minutes

National Literacy Strategy links

Year 4 Term 3 T14: 'to write poems, experimenting with different styles and structures'

Group size

2–4

Equipment

Pen; paper; collection of books about the chosen subject

Introduction

Xeransis literally means 'drying up', and to play the game pupils need to write a piece that 'dries up'. In so doing it loses a word from each line until only a single word remains. Although Xeransis is not strictly a poetry-writing game, it does facilitate play with language and the manipulation of text – two key aspects in the development of poetry writing.

How to play

The game is explained, as in the introduction. The teacher also explains that the object of the game is to write the most interesting or unusual poem.

The class (or large group) are then asked to make up six sentences about a predetermined subject, such as food. The teacher needs to indicate that they do not need to worry about the number of words they use.

The teacher (or pupil scribe) writes the six suggestions so that they can easily be seen by all.

The number of words in each sentence is then counted, e.g:

I like spicy food (4)
I eat Chinese food with chopsticks (6)
I prefer savoury to sweet food (6)
Eating is fun (3)
I need a drink with a meal (7)
I usually have sandwiches for lunch (6)

The longest sentence is then picked out (*I need a drink with a meal*) and written on a separate part of the writing surface.

The teacher explains that this will be the first sentence of the finished Xeransis and then asks how many words long the next sentence should be (6 words).

Sentences from the original list can then be used and/or adapted (made longer or shorter) to complete the poem so that each successive line has one less word e.g:

I need a drink with a meal (7)
I prefer savoury to sweet food (6)
I eat sandwiches for lunch (5)
I like spicy food (4)
Eating is fun (3)
Look, chopsticks (2)
YUM! (1)

Once the process has been successfully modelled pupils are divided into groups of 2–4 to collaboratively write their own Xeransis on a given theme.

After completion interesting/unusual examples are chosen for display and praise. The teacher may, or may not, wish to describe these as 'winners'.

Extension activity

For quick finishers (and/or more able pupils), the poem can continue and expand so that after the final single word line it grows again until the length of the original sentence is reached once more.

Paragraphs and Key Ideas

Main idea

To help pupils focus on the key aspects of texts

How long?

20 minutes

National Literacy Strategy links

Year 4 Term 3 T24: 'to summarise in writing the key ideas from, e.g. a paragraph or chapter'

Group size

Pairs

Equipment

Pen; paper; two envelopes for each pair (one marked 'Paragraphs' the other 'Key Ideas'); a selection of six paragraphs in one envelope and six blank sheets of paper in the other

Introduction

The game encourages pupils to discuss and identify the key ideas from more extended pieces of writing.

The results from the game can be used as an effective gauge of a pupil's ability to identify the key idea/s of a paragraph.

How to play

Pupils are divided into pairs.

Each pair is given two envelopes. One is labelled 'Paragraphs' (see examples); the other 'Key Ideas'. In the first envelope there are a number of paragraphs, each written on a separate sheet of paper. In the other there are the same number of blank sheets of paper.

The pupils are asked to tip out the contents of their two envelopes into two piles.

They are then asked to write a key idea which matches each paragraph in a specified period of time (20 minutes usually suffices).

The 'winning' pair have the most accurate key ideas.

Extension activities

The game can obviously be made more complex by altering the level of difficulty or readability of the chosen paragraphs. A further variant is 'Headlines for Newspaper Articles' in which pupils are given articles for which they have to suggest headlines.

Examples

Tudor Schools

PARAGRAPHS	KEY IDEAS
In Tudor times school breaks were not like ours today. There were, in fact no summer holidays at all, although schools did close at Christmas and Easter.	Tudor children didn't have as many school holidays as we have today.
You did not have a biro or pencil but instead you wrote with a feather you'd sharpened with a knife. It made a scratching noise as you wrote with it.	Writing tools were different.
Most children didn't go to school at all. A small number went to 'Dame' schools which were run by a local lady. Only children from richer families could be sent to school. Until Henry VIII closed the monasteries these were called church schools.	You were lucky if you went to school at all!
Tudor schools were very strict. You were beaten for leaning on the table and you would be beaten for losing your school cap. If you said a rude word you would be caned three times.	Tudor schools were very strict.
The job of a teacher was not just to help pupils with work. They also had to check that pupils had washed and that they behaved properly, both in church and school. They also had to make sure that pupils combed their hair!	Teachers were more than just educators.

Haikuzation

Main idea

To isolate the main parts of a story and reproduce these as a Haiku, thereby reinforcing Haiku writing

How long?

20–25 minutes

National Literacy Strategy links

Year 5 Term 1 T16: 'to convey feelings, reflections or moods in a poem through the careful choice of words and phrases'

Group size

Pairs

Equipment

Pen; paper; examples of fairy tales or simple books

Introduction

A Haiku is a Japanese syllabic form which is (often) three lines long. The first line has five syllables, the second seven and the third five. A good Haiku distils the moment and captures the essence of that moment. In this game the purpose is to produce a Haiku from a longer poem or story so as to capture the main meaning, feeling and mood of the original text.

Syllabification is one of the spelling strategies which pupils can use and this game can be used to embed the strategy.

How to play

Pupils are divided into pairs.

The teacher explains what a Haiku is, using the information above.

Haikuzation is then explained – producing a Haiku from a longer poem or story.

One or two examples are shown to the class or group and discussed. The examples provided at the end of this section should provide a useful basis for such discussion.

The class/group then write a Haiku collectively.

The teacher then explains that the purpose of the game is to produce the most interesting Haikuzations! To further motivate pupils the teacher could explain that a class book of Haikuzations will be made and/or the most interesting examples will be displayed on the 'Work of Special Merit' board etc.

The pupils are given a list of fairy tales, familiar texts, or familiar poems to work on. Good examples include Puss in Boots, The Sleeping Beauty, Rapunzel, and The Emperor's New Clothes.

After approximately 20–25 minutes the work is collected and marked.

The 'winning' examples are displayed/praised with due ceremony.

Extension activity

Should pupils find the brevity of the Haiku difficult to operate with then it may be preferable to offer a Tanka as an alternative. This is another Japanese form, five lines long, whose syllabic pattern is 5, 7, 5, 7, 7.

Examples of Haiku

1 *Little Red Riding Hood*
   ... Goes to see grandma,
   Meets wolf. Woodcutter kills it,
   Grandma saved ... Hurrah!

2 *Cinderella*
   Pretty sister slave
   Her wish is granted – Magic!
   Prince's love she wins.

3 *Three Little Pigs*
   Pig brothers build homes
   Of straw, wood and brick; wolf blows
   Each down ... brick survives!

Add-a-Word (and words between)

Main idea

To vary sentence construction through a games format.

How long?

5–10 minutes

National Literacy Strategy links

By using this form of questioning the teacher can make an explicit link with the *Year 5 Term 1 W10 objective:* 'to use adverbs to qualify verbs in writing dialogue ...'; *Year 5 Term 3 S3:* 'to search for, identify and classify a range of prepositions: *back, up, down, across, through, on, etc* ...'

Group size

Any size (can be a whole class game); 3–5 for extension activity

Equipment

The main game does not require the pupils to use any equipment

Introduction

The idea of this game is to expand sentences by adding more words to them.

When introducing 'Add-a-word' the teacher should begin with a base sentence of twelve or more words. The theme is unimportant but opportunities to link the subject matter of the sentence to material being taught in the class should be capitalised upon. The following example shows how the game works.

How to play

The teacher writes a sentence of twelve or more words on the board, e.g:

> *He walked along the road to meet his friend, a tall man called Bob.*

The sentence is written by the teacher so that it is visible to all pupils taking part.

The teacher then asks a series of progressively more complex questions, all of which require words to be added to the sentence, e.g:

'Can you add-a-word anywhere in the sentence?'

'Can you add-a-word between 'X' and 'X'?' (Reduce the number of words to about half the original sentence, e.g. between 'meet' and 'Bob')

'Can you add a two syllable word anywhere in the sentence?'

'Can you add a word of more than two syllables anywhere in the sentence?'

'Can you add an adverb after *walked* to qualify it?'

Many teaching points arise naturally from this game, such as the use of the comma to separate words in a list. It is also a useful (and fun!) way of reinforcing the explicit teaching of many aspects of sentence level work such as active and passive verbs.

Extension activity

An interesting variant on the basic Add-a-word game is 'Words Between'. The teacher begins by writing five words so that they are visible to all participating pupils. Pupils, in groups, then have to add words between these five words so as to produce a sentence. If groups work at varying paces it is best to offer additional sets of starter words as extension activities. If the five words are carefully chosen, e.g. *up, down, across, through, on,* then sentence level work objectives can be reinforced. A finished example using these five words could read:

> *Up above the village, down by the wood, across a path and through a field was where John walked before continuing on to the old house.*

Onomatopoeia

Main idea

To improve pupils' understanding of onomatopoeia by exploring words that imitate sounds

How long?

20–25 minutes

National Literacy Strategy links

Year 5 Term 2 W11: 'to explore onomatopoeia. Collect, invent and use words whose meaning is represented in their sounds, e.g. *splash, plop, bang, clash, smack, tickle, swoop'*

Group size

Pairs

Equipment

Pen; paper; dictionaries; photocopy of 'The Onomatopeic A–Z Challenge' (page 61)

Introduction

Onomatopoeia is the formation of words that imitate a noise or action, such as *hiss, plop, clang.* The 'A–Z challenge' is a simple game to explain but demands thought from the pupils.

How to play

Pupils are divided into pairs.

Each pair is given a photocopy of the A–Z Challenge sheet on which the alphabet is written vertically.

The teacher explains that the object of the game is to complete the sheet using as many onomatopoeic words as possible within a given time limit (approximately 20 minutes is usually sufficient). If the pupils need further explanation a video of the 1960s' Batman series works superbly – think 'POW', 'SOCK', etc.!

The teacher stresses that there is no need to complete the sheet in alphabetical order.

When the time has elapsed teams swap sheets and a score is awarded according to how many were completed.

The winning team is announced. (The teacher should take great care to avoid stigmatising those who found the game difficult e.g. avoid selecting a winner by asking 'Who scored 1?' 'Who scored 2?' etc. as this shows the whole class who had the worst score.)

Extension activity

'Plop went ...' is another time-limited game in which children have to write as many phrases as possible beginning with 'Plop went...' e.g. 'Plop went the frog as it hopped into the water.'

The starting point for this game can be varied by the substitution of other onomatopoeic words.

The Onomatopoeic A–Z Challenge

| Name | _____ | Date | _____ |

a	
b	
c	
d	
e	
f	
g	
h	
i	
j	
k	
l	
m	
n	
o	
p	
q	
r	
s	
t	
u	
v	
w	
x	
y	
z	

The 11 Syllable Challenge (Hendecasyllabics)

Main idea

To reinforce and embed understanding of synonyms, and show how to find them in a thesaurus

How long?

15–20 minutes

National Literacy Strategy links

Year 5 Term 3 W11: 'to use a range of dictionaries and understand their purposes, e.g. dictionaries of slang, phrases, idioms, contemporary usage, synonyms, antonyms, quotations, and thesauruses'

Group size

Pairs

Equipment

Pen; paper; thesaurus; dictionary

Introduction

The game encourages pupils to explore syllables and ultimately write 11-syllable long sentences or definitions. A Hendecasyllabic is an 11-syllable line, originally used by ancient Roman poets (such as Catullus) as a way of formally organising their poetry. As a word game this challenge encourages pupils to think carefully about the vocabulary they are using.

How to play

Pupils are divided into pairs.

The teacher shows examples of Hendecasyllabic sentences such as these:

Gladiator: Slave fighter, in the arena dies by sword
Water: We drink it, swim in it, sail on its surface
Wind: It can be a breeze or whirling tornado

The concept of syllables is discussed/reinforced and the 11-syllable sentence is explained as per the Introduction.

The teacher introduces a list of subjects or themes or, better still, encourages the pupils to do so.

The class is asked to provide a brief spoken description of each subject or theme.

The teacher writes the pupils' descriptions on a surface that can be seen by all the class.

With the help of the class the number of syllables in each description is counted.

If the syllable count is below 11, the teacher asks for additional words and phrases to bring the number to 11. Should there be more than 11, then the teacher asks for suggestions as to how the sentence might be shortened.

The pupils are then given a further list of unusual subjects or ones which are related to work being undertaken in the class.

A time limit of approximately 15–20 minutes is set for the production of as many 11-syllable sentences as possible.

Thesauruses are handed out and pupils are encouraged to find longer or shorter synonyms for words written down in their first drafts.

After completion and marking, excellent examples are displayed, certificates awarded etc.

Lipograms

Main idea

To use a thesaurus in a meaningful context which is not worksheet-driven

How long?

30–45 minutes

National Literacy Strategy links

Year 5 Term 3 W11: 'to use a range of dictionaries and understand their purposes, e.g. ... thesauruses'

Group size

Pairs

Equipment

Pen; paper; thesaurus

Introduction

A lipogram is a piece of writing which is completed without using a specified letter.

How to play

The teacher introduces the game in a dramatic manner, e.g. 'I am the President of Letterland and today I have decided to ban the use of the letter 'O' . If you use it once you will be fined £5, if you use it twice you will be fined £10 and for the third offence you will suffer an immediate beheading. I would now like you to write a story about worms.'

The pupils are then asked to begin writing in pairs. This usually elicits a response along the lines of 'But worms has an 'o' in it!' so providing the opportunity to discuss synonyms and replacement phrases. If the pupils don't question the situation the teacher asks 'What's the problem?'

Now, as a class, pupils are asked to provide a phrase which could replace 'worms'. The teacher can then use questioning to refine the initial responses.

Teacher: Can anyone suggest a phrase that could be used to replace worms? Don't forget that it has not got to include the letter 'O'.

Pupil X: Wriggling thing.

Teacher: Good attempt, but could a wriggling thing be something other than a worm, for example a snake?

Pupil X: Yes.

Teacher: So can you make wriggling thing more precise?

Pupil X: Small wriggling thing that lives under the grass.

Teacher: Excellent answer.

This technique, utilising careful questioning, helps pupils to take a considered approach to the vocabulary they are using.

Now that the game has been discussed pupils return to writing in pairs. Thesauruses are provided as an aid to writing, and their use can be discussed. The winning pair are those who produce the longest piece of writing (without using the specified letter!) within a specified time limit.

Extension activity

As an extension activity, pupils can be given a modelled example of a sentence with a banned letter, in this instance 'O', e.g. 'It's better playing games inside when it's wet because it is frightfully disgusting feeling drenched in the rain!' Pupils are then asked to write improved versions, or to write on the same theme ('P.E. in the rain'), omitting a different letter such as 'u' or 'i'. (Avoid banning the letter 'e' except with the most able pupils.)

Palindromes

Main idea

To explore patterns within words in a 'games' context

How long?

15 minutes for the production of palindrones and palindrome-riddles, and up to 20 further minutes for sharing riddles and guessing palindromes

National Literacy Strategy links

Year 5 Term 3 W12: 'to use dictionaries efficiently to explore spellings, meanings, derivations, e.g. by using alphabetical order, abbreviations, definitions with understanding'

Group size

4–6

Equipment

Pen; paper; dictionaries

Introduction

A palindrome is a word or phrase which, when read in reverse order, is the same. Some examples of palindromes are: *bib, dad, deed, did, gag, gig, mum, noon, peep, pip, sees, toot, wow.*

How to play

Pupils are divided into groups of 4–6.

The teacher introduces the concept of a palindrome and shares one or two examples of palindromic words, introducing a 'games' element by giving pupils riddles for each word e.g.

I am a small seed found in an apple. What am I? (pip)

I am worn by a baby to stop food spilling on its clothes. What am I? (bib)

I am a short word for father. What am I? (dad)

Once the pupils have an understanding of palindromes they are given 15 minutes to list as many as possible, and produce riddles for them. They are provided with dictionaries in order to find a range of examples. Teams are then asked to present their riddles to the class.

The winning team are those judged to have the best palindromes and riddles at the end of the 15 minute period.

Extension activity

A useful extension activity is to ask pupils to use as many
palindromes as possible in a short story. (The pupils may wish to
suggest titles or the teacher may prefer to start with titles that
have proved successful in workshops. These include, 'The day
my school went mad'; 'My best friend's an alien'; 'The world's
worst vampire'.) The palindromes should be underlined in a
different colour so that the number used can be easily
ascertained.

Flash Fiction

Main idea

To write collaboratively with a deadline

How long?

20–30 mins

National Literacy Strategy links

Year 6 Term 2 T13: 'to use different genres as models to write ...'

Group size

Pairs or groups of 3 or 4

Equipment

Pen; paper; example of 'flash fiction'

Introduction

This is a writing game which is currently gaining international popularity with competitions being organised on a regular basis. A piece of 'Flash Fiction' is a story told in a specified number of words; the number used in most competitions is 50 and this is a good number to use when working with pupils. (If the teacher wishes to simplify the activity a target of between 40 and 60 words can be set.)

How to play

Pupils are shown an example of Flash Fiction.

> *I became Cinderella's coachman. It was much better than living down a sewer. At midnight, however, I had a tail and four legs again ... but I kept my human voice! Humans, unfortunately, didn't like me as I didn't look like them and rats hated me as I'd lost my squeak!*

The idea of a very short story with a Beginning, Middle and Ending is introduced.

The rule that it should include a problem is made clear.

The importance of an element of surprise is also discussed.

Pupils then choose their own theme and in their teams produce a piece of flash fiction within the deadline of 20–30 minutes. Winning examples are selected by the class.

Extension activities

There are three useful extension activities:

1 Pupils are given a theme such as 'The worst storm ever' (any phrase beginning 'The worst …' works well) and in pairs or groups of three or four are asked to write a story, in exactly 50 words, about the given theme. A fixed time limit of 20–30 minutes works well.

2 Pupils are given the title of a familiar work of fiction such as *Cinderella* and are invited to rewrite it in 50 words.

3 After a shared reading session pupils are asked to rewrite what they have just read as a piece of Flash Fiction.

Each of the above activities has its own benefits:

Activity 1: Drafting is encouraged as pupils rarely complete the work within the time limit. The drafting therefore has a real purpose and is not seen as a 'writing up in neat' exercise.

Activity 2: This is useful as a diagnostic and allows the teacher to assess the pupils ability to précis a work. With less able children preliminary work may need to be undertaken in order to show them how to eliminate unnecessary words and also how to select key events/points in the original text.

Activity 3: The teacher has immediate feedback regarding pupils' understanding or comprehension of what has just been read. The pupils' understanding is increased by 'processing' the text that has just been read and the content of that text is more likely to enter long term memory.

When the time limit is over the most exciting examples are chosen as winners.

Word Inventor

Main idea

To encourage dictionary use as a part of creative play with language, and to encourage discussion of words

How long?

30–40 minutes (in total)

National Literacy Strategy links

Year 6 Term 3 W5: 'to invent words using known roots, prefixes and suffixes'

Group size

2–4

Equipment

Pen; paper; dictionaries; photocopies of Word Inventor sheets (page 72)

Introduction

The game encourages pupils to invent new words by combining two (or more) words that already exist. Numerous examples of word combination occur in the English language, including *smog* – a blend of smoke and fog; *brunch* – a combination of breakfast and lunch; *moped* – an amalgam of motor and pedal; *motel* – a fusion of motor and hotel.

How to play

Pupils are divided into groups of two to four.

Word invention is explained and the examples included in the introduction are discussed. Pupils can be invited to provide other examples that they know.

The teacher annouces dramatically that today the class is going to improve the English Dictionary by adding some of their own words.

The pupils are then given an example of an invented word and its possible definitions are then discussed. e.g. *Wedry* – a day of changing weather, a combination of wet and dry.

Pupils are then asked to invent their own words. They number these and write them on a sheet of paper. A separate numbered sheet is used for their definitions.

After approximately 20 minutes groups swap their word lists and try to guess the intended meaning.

After 10 minutes of discussion the original groups of pupils then invent further portmanteau words and their accompanying definitions. These can be written on to the photocopiable sheet provided. (The third column 'Between which two words in the dictionary?' is optional. It can provide an extra tier of challenge for more able pupils and also serves to reinforce second and third letter alphabetical ordering.)

Extension activity

A more complex method of playing Word Inventor is to begin with definitions (see examples below) and then to ask pupils to invent appropriate new words.

Examples

Characters
Someone who is mainly shy but can sometimes be loud
Someone who pretends to be kind but is really cruel
Someone who hops and skips instead of walking
Someone who laughs and cries.

Weather
A cloudy then clear day
A windy then still day
A hot and cold day
A snowy and blustery day
A dusty and dry day

Word Inventor

Name _____	Date _____

My words	Definitions	Between which two words in dictionary

Rally

Main idea

To extend pupils vocabulary and improve spelling

How long?

10–15 minutes (15–20 minutes for the themed extension activity)

National Literacy Strategy links

Year 6 Term 3 W3: 'to use independent spelling strategies ...'

Group size

Pairs

Equipment

Pen; paper

Introduction

Rally is an excellent brainstorming activity where a list of words is produced in which the last two letters of each word in the list form the first two of the following word.

How to play

The teacher asks for a word beginning with 'X' (any other letter of the alphabet will do!)

When a word has been suggested the children have to suggest another word, which begins with the last two letters of the opening word. The pattern is continued until the Rally can no longer be extended, or time runs out.

If the opening word were 'table' a sequence might be
    TABLE
    LEAP
    APE
    PEN

The pupils are then asked to suggest two or three different opening words and produce their own Rally using these.

The winning pair produce the longest Rally in a deadlined period.

Extension activity

The game is itself a useful method of differentiating 'Staircase' (page 13)

To make Rally more difficult the game can be themed, e.g. the teacher introduces a theme such as 'Buildings' . The pupils continue the Rally with words associated with that theme, e.g.

FLAT
ATTIC
ICE-HOUSE

It is worth spending time teaching the children strategies to use if they become stuck, e.g. if the above rally had begun: Shop – Opera House, and no words beginning with 'se ' related to the topic, could be thought of; they could *either* (a) alter the second word by thinking of another beginning with 'op', *or* (b) use a book about the subject and look in the index and/or glossary to try and find a suitable word.

If they are producing a Rally on an unfamiliar subject, or indeed a familiar one with unusual possibilities, it is advisable to explain that in order to score points they must be able to explain the meaning of each word used in their Rally.

Acrostic Detectives

Main idea

To vary the sometimes 'overused' acrostic form

How long?

25–35 minutes

National Literacy Strategy links

Year 6 Term 3 W6: 'to practise and extend vocabulary e.g. through inventing word games such as puns, riddles, crosswords.

Group size

Pairs

Equipment

Pen; paper; dictionaries; selection of books related to the chosen theme word

Introduction

To play Acrostic Detectives pupils need an understanding of the Acrostic, a poem in which a theme word is chosen and written vertically on the page.The letters of the 'theme word' act as the first letter of each line of the poem (which must be about the theme word); an Acrostic whose theme word is 'Food' could therefore read:

Fried food is fine tasting
Old fashioned fish and chips
Oh, how that makes my mouth water-
Delicious cod in a nice crisp batter!

If the pupils have never written Acrostics before it would be advisable to attempt one or two of these before progressing to Acrostic Detectives.

How to play

The teacher, or pupils, choose a theme word. This could be related to something being taught in class or could be chosen purely for fun.

The pupils are divided into pairs.

The teacher explains that the letters of the 'theme word' can be hidden anywhere in the line, the only rule being that it should be hidden in the same place in each line of the Acrostic, e.g. if the first letter of the theme word is the second letter of line one, then the second letter of the theme word must be the second letter of line two, and so on.

The teacher shows a modelled example (see example).

Working in pairs, the pupils write their Hidden Acrostic according to the rule given above.

When the Hidden Acrostics are complete each pair swaps with another and searches for the rule that the others have used (e.g. the other team's 'theme word' is hidden in the second letter of each line). To complete the game this rule is written under the Hidden Acrostic.

The winning team is the first to write down the rule which the other team has used.

Extension activity

For more able pupils an Acrostic Detective challenge may be set by the teacher. The aim is to 'Beat the Teacher!', a sure-fire motivator. There are innumerable possibilities including:

Can you hide an Acrostic in the first letter of the adverb used in each line?

Can you hide an Acrostic in the last letter of the word before the verb in each line?

(If these challenges are proposed, the teacher should ask pupils to use only one adverb or verb on each line of their poem!)

Example

Often fried food tastes fine
Long ago, fish and chips were wrapped in newspaper
Too many years have passed since I last ate such a supper
Edible meals are O.K. but delicious ones are better!!

(Here the 'theme word' is hidden as the second letter of each line.)

Glidograms

Main idea

To extend vocabulary through the medium of a word game

How long?

15–25 minutes

National Literacy Strategy links

Year 6 Term 3 W6: 'to practise and extend vocabulary, e.g. through inventing word games such as puns, riddles, crosswords'

Group size

Pairs

Equipment

Pen; paper; photocopies of 'Glidogram Frames' (page 80)

Introduction

A Glidogram consists of seven words, written as a list, each of which contains a specific letter. The first word begins with the chosen letter, the second word has the letter placed second in the word and so forth until the fourth word after which the letter slides back to the original position. The beauty of glidograms is that they can be adapted to any curricular area. They also encourage pupils to skim and scan related books.

A glidogram using *a* as the focus letter could read as follows:

> *a*nt
> b*a*g
> br*a*in
> str*a*nge
> cl*a*m
> d*a*rk
> *a*sk

How to play

The concept of the Glidogram is explained by the teacher.

The base for a Glidogram is then written for all to see, with the correct number of gaps before the chosen letter e.g.

a _____

_ *a* _____

_ _ *a* _____

_ *a* _____

a _____

The teacher then asks for a word beginning with *a*. The first line is then completed.

The process outlined in the introduction is continued until the Glidogram is complete.

Now that the Glidogram has been modelled the pupils are divided into pairs and each pair is given a photocopied base sheet with a chosen letter.

Pupils are then given 15 minutes in which to write as many Glidograms as possible for their letter.

In order to avoid meaningless copying the teacher needs to point out that they must be able to explain the meaning of all the words they have used.

At the end of the time limit winners are selected.

Extension activities

Themed Glidograms are more complex than the open activity described above. To play this the teacher gives the Glidogram a title ('Food' will do once again!) and suggests clues, e.g.

The first word I am thinking of is a kind of fruit (*apple*)

The second word I'm thinking of accompanies pepper (*salt*)

The third word I'm thinking of comes in bunches (*grapes*)

The fourth word is yellow and bendy (*banana*)

The fifth word is also a kind of fruit which is narrow at the top and wide at the bottom (*pear*)

The sixth word looks like a small orange (*tangerine*)

The final word is a fruit with a velvety skin (*apricot*)

An alternative to the themed approach is to use the Glidogram to reinforce understanding of parts of speech. In workshops I encourage children to produce a Glidogram of 'Adjectives to describe a person'. A letter *e* example might read:

*e*xceptional

b*e*autiful

sp*e*cial

ecc*e*ntric

pr*e*tty

d*e*lightful

*e*ducated

Pupils are later asked to use these adjectives in the context of a narrative piece of writing whose particular focus is characterisation.

The easiest Glidograms are produced with the vowels as their focus letter. Grids for these are provided over the page.

Glidogram Frame – Letter 'a'

Name _____ **Date** _____

Title 1 _____

a								
	a							
		a						
			a					
		a						
	a							
a								

Title 2 _____

a								
	a							
		a						
			a					
		a						
	a							
a								

Glidogram Frame – Letter 'e'

Name _____ Date _____

Title 1 _____

e									
	e								
		e							
			e						
		e							
	e								
e									

Title 2 _____

e									
	e								
		e							
			e						
		e							
	e								
e									

81

Glidogram Frame – Letter 'i'

Name _____ Date _____

Title 1 _____

i								
	i							
		i						
			i					
		i						
	i							
i								

Title 2 _____

i								
	i							
		i						
			i					
		i						
	i							
i								

Glidogram Frame – Letter 'o'

Name _____ **Date** _____

Title 1 _____

o									
	o								
		o							
			o						
		o							
	o								
o									

Title 2 _____

o									
	o								
		o							
			o						
		o							
	o								
o									

Glidogram Frame – Letter 'u'

Name _____ Date _____

Title 1 _____

u									
	u								
		u							
			u						
	u								
	u								
u									

Title 2 _____

u									
	u								
		u							
			u						
		u							
	u								
u									

The Rebus Game

Main idea

To 'play' with language

How long?

15–25 minutes

National Literacy Strategy links

Year 6 Term 3 W7: 'to experiment with language ...'

Group size

Pairs

Equipment

Pen; paper; dictionaries

Introduction

A Rebus is a sentence, paragraph or story in which some of the words have been replaced with either one or a combination of the following: (a) Letters; (b) Pictures; (c) Numbers.

How to play

Pupils are divided into pairs.

The teacher shows the pupils an example of a Rebus e.g.

U R 2 GOOD 2  TRUE

The teacher then explains that, in order to produce a Rebus, words (or parts of words) are replaced by letters, pictures or numbers.

Pupils are then invited to produce either a number or letter Rebus for the following words, which the teacher writes for all to see.

Ate (8)

Are (R)

You (U)

If the pupils cope easily with this then the teacher writes words that require letter combinations e.g.

tear (TR)

(See 'Examples' for further words and their Rebus replacements.)

When the concept of a Rebus has been grasped pupils are given 15–25 minutes to write their own Rebus sentences.

At the end of the alloted time pairs swap their work and each tries to 'decode' the other's Rebus. The 'decoded' version is written beneath the original (or on a separate sheet of paper).

Examples are shared and discussed.

Extension activity

If pupils manage the main Rebus game, described above, they can be introduced to the more complex approach in which a pictogram with letters crossed out is used to indicate a word. This is best explained by example:

Pairs who have been taught this approach can then produce a more complex Rebus for decoding.

Examples

Letters		Numbers	
Word	*Rebus equivalent*		*Rebus equivalent*
Be/Bee	B	Won	1
See/Sea	C	Too/To	2
Eye	I	For/Fore	4
Jay (the bird)	J	*Letter combinations*	
Oh!	O	*Word*	*Rebus equivalent*
Pea	P	Arty	RT
Cue/Queue	Q	Icy	IC
Tee/Tea	T	Tear	TR
Why	Y	Cure	QR

Defect Detectives

Main idea

To reinforce aspects of literacy such as capital letters, and to correct spellings in an enjoyable manner

How long?

15–20 minutes

National Literacy Strategy links

Numerous, depending upon chosen focus

Group size

Pairs

Equipment

Pen; paper; copies of the sheets associated with this game (pages 89–91)

Introduction

Defect Detectives is a game in which children hunt for mistakes. Much of its success, therefore, lies in the ability of the teacher to dramatise the game's introduction. Rewards such as 'Head Detective' badges or certificates also seem to increase pupils' levels of motivation. Three photocopiable examples have been provided: 'Spot the missing punctuation!', 'Spot the spelling mistakes!' and 'Spot the missing Capital Letters!' These pre-prepared texts include a broad range of defects such as common spelling errors (said/sed) and homophone errors (too/to) etc.

The Capital Letters sheet omits capitals at the start of sentences, the first person pronoun, days of the month, place names etc. The Missing Punctuation sheet omits full stops, commas, question marks, speech marks and apostrophes.

These can easily be adapted so that any number of National Literacy Strategy objectives are met – word usage, grammar and punctuation spring to mind!

The author has found this game to be especially useful when introducing the concept of paragraphs. In this instance it is necessary to stress that a new paragraph occurs when there is a change of time, place, speaker or focus.

How to play

The pupils are divided into pairs.

The teacher dramatically introduces the game, explaining the meaning of the word 'defect' in order to avoid confusion.

The pupils are set a deadline for using their Detective Powers to find as many errors as possible in the passage provided.

One or other of the examples provided may be used or the teacher may wish to write his/her own. The passage is handed out with much ceremony, e.g. 'Don't turn it over until we have completed our special detective countdown … 10, 9, 8, 7, 6, 5, 4, 3, 2, 1 … Begin!'

When the time has elapsed pupils discuss the mistakes they have found. (It is useful to use an OHT of the passage which can be corrected for all to see.)

When all the mistakes have been corrected pupils mark their own work.

The winners are given a 'Head Detective' badge or certificate.

Extension activity

Pupils, working in groups of four, prepare a defective passage for other groups to solve. This can have one error type or a range of error types for added difficulty. The different types of error should be specified at the top of the page e.g. spelling and punctuation.

Spot the missing punctuation!

One warm sunny day I went to my sisters house She was in

the garden

I said Hello

She replied How are you

It was good to see her We sat down by the roses and she

pointed to a tree

Its lovely isnt it she said

I nodded as I hadnt seen anything as beautiful in years It

was a great afternoon Have you ever had one like it

Spot the spelling mistakes!

The wurst ever trip to the libray

I woke up erly and new that i hadn't remembed something.

it was my libray buks. I shud hav taken them bak yesterday

but it had sliped my mind. I supose I was just to busy.

I drest quikly and rusht of with moar buks than you can

imagine.Wen I arrived I walkt up too the counter and sed

'Were can I pay my fyne?'

The librarean was very kind. She sed that this time it didn't

mater. I felt so hapy that I ran home, lafing all the way.

Spot the missing Capital Letters!

It was early when i found the little dog in the street. It was just outside of number 10 arlington avenue. I noticed that it had a broken leg and had no idea how this had happened. perhaps it was the result of someone being cruel? Well, i decided to take it to the r.s.p.c.a. so i knocked on Mr and mrs jones' door and asked if john could come along and help me. We carefully placed the puppy in a box and carried it half way across newcastle. It looked very sad! The person at the r.s.p.c.a. was very pleased. He thanked us and asked to come back 2 weeks later, in early october, to see how it was getting on. We left feeling very pleased and that night told mr. wheeler, the shopkeeper down the road, exactly what we had done. He said he was very proud of us.

The Very Secret Word Game

Main idea

To embed word level aspects of language such as understanding of verbs, adverbs, adjectives etc

How long?

15 minutes

National Literacy Strategy links

Numerous according to the rules used

Group size

Pairs

Equipment

Pen; paper

Introduction

The game encourages pupils to play with language by using rules to hide a short sentence within a longer passage of text. 'Today we are going to be spies!' is a good child-friendly way to introduce this game to pupils.

How to play

The class are asked to think of a short sentence which a spy might write, e.g. 'Meet me at midnight.'

They are then told the special spy rule that each word of the initial sentence must be preceded by *and.*

They are then shown how to apply this rule so as to hide the initial sentence in a longer passage of writing.

The following example is an expanded version of 'Meet me at midnight'.

*When you telephoned to ask me to come **and** meet in the cafe I felt happy. I was glad that you also felt happy. It was kind, the way you asked after Jenny **and** me. We drank a glass of lemonade **and** at first talked very little. Then time raced **and** midnight came too quickly.*

Now that the process has been modelled the pupils are divided into pairs and given four or five sentences to hide.

A 15 minute deadline works well.

Extension activities

There are many alternatives to the above playing method. For example, the coded message could be hidden after each adjective used in the longer passage, or after numbers etc.

It proves a popular game with pupils especially when they have a partner who has to crack their coded message!

Word Deletion Games

Main idea

To promote reading-for-meaning and inferential understanding of text

How long?

30 minutes

National Literacy Strategy links

The activity can be related to a broad range of reading comprehension objectives; it improves comprehension by encouraging close, active reading of texts.

Group size

2–4

Equipment

Pen; paper; copies of a passage of text with a section deleted (see page 96)

Introduction

Word Deletion is, effectively, a form of cloze procedure. Most cloze exercises, however, only omit single words. In this game whole sentences and paragraphs are also omitted. The advantage over single word cloze procedures is that it promotes inferential reading skills.

How to play

Discussion should be actively encouraged when playing this game.

The class is divided into groups of 2–4.

The teacher hands each group a passage of text with sections missing. An indication should be made as to how much text is missing from each gap, e.g.(*1 sentence*); (*5 sentences*); (*4 words*); (*a 7 sentence paragraph*); etc.

The teacher explains that the purpose of the game is to guess what is missing from the gaps and to write down their version of what they think is missing.

Pupils then have a time-limited period to complete the unfinished text. (In order for the pupils to perceive this as more of a game it is useful to dramatise the introduction ... 'Pens poised... Are you ready?' etc.)

At the end of the allotted time groups show their versions and explain why they think their words and sentences are correct.

After all the groups have shown their work the teacher shows the original.

At this point the 'sense' of pupils' attempts should be praised so that they are don't become disheartened at not being word perfect.

Extension activity

The game can be played in foundation subjects with extra books available on the chosen subject in order to help pupils to complete the missing sections (which are subject specific).

Possible answers to deletion exercise (attempts which are sensible and can be justified are just as good!)

1 word: record

5 words: enormous lump of chewing gum

3 words: flapping their arms

14 words: very odd looking creatures from outer space to replace teachers at their school

3 words: Early flying skills

20 word sentence: No-one in the gang could fly and no-one in the gang knew the names of the creatures in the zoo!

Word deletion

Billy's gang had been together now for more than two weeks. This
was quite a _____ (1 word) and Billy was very proud of it. You
could tell by the way he walked around in the playgropund, head up
in the air with an _____ (5 words)
stuck in his mouth.

Billy's gang followed behind him.

Everyone knew about them: they were brave, they were strong, they
were afraid of nothing. The stories in the playground grew wilder as
the days passed. On Monday Billy's gang were rumoured to be the
fastest runners in the whole school. By Wednesday they could fly
through the air without even _____ (3 words).
On Thursday everyone was whispering about the spacecraft they'd
built with their bare hands. They were about to help some _____

_____

_____ (14 words).

The teachers were all going to be beamed up to a deep, dark dungeon
on the alien's planet after which lessons would consist of 'Space
Travel' in the Juniors and _____ (3 words) in
the Infants. The whole school was very excited at the idea of their
teachers being swapped for aliens, all except Mike.

Mike was one of Bill's gang and he knew none of the stories was true.

_____

_____

_____ . (20 word sentence)